Vicuña

Loro Piana

Vicuña

THE QUEEN OF THE ANDES

Photographs by
Bruna Rotunno

SKIRA

The story of the vicuña is closely connected to both our personal story and business history. It began with our love of beauty and our father Franco's passion for the world's finest fibers. In the 1950s and 1960s, before the vicuña was classified as a protected species, our father dealt with the fleece, captivated by its extraordinary softness and lightness. And so it was that we learnt about vicuñas and our passion for their story began.

In 1976, in an effort to safeguard the animals from extinction, the Washington Convention banned vicuña fiber trading. Led by our passion for a fiber that has no equals in the animal kingdom, and attracted by the possibility of becoming part of the preservation of these diminutive members of the camel family, we seized the moment and started working to protect the animals.

In the mid-1980s, in partnership with the Peruvian government, our company's first attempts to set up repopulation centres were not successful. Subsequently, we continued to collaborate with the authorities to explore solutions that would benefit the local communities while discouraging poaching. We then found that the answer lay in the reintroduction of the fiber onto the market, on condition that it was obtained exclusively from shearing live animals. The *campesinos* were now entrusted with the care of the small camelids and compensated for their fleeces.

Heading a consortium in 1994, we were granted the exclusive rights to purchase the entire annual production of vicuña fiber, and employ it to craft products of outstanding excellence. Since then we have always remained firmly committed to safeguarding the species while continuing to tell the tragic story of the vicuña, brought close to extinction by human greed, and eager to find new ways to do more.

In 2008, our allegiance to the vicuñas led to the creation of the reserve named after our father Franco, where the number of animals continues to rise under the vigilant eyes of the local wardens.

Recently, we ventured beyond Peru, into the icy uplands of northern Argentina, where we have a majority holding in a company that has the rights to an area where more than 4,500 vicuñas live wild, protected from poachers and constantly monitored by veterinarians and experienced personnel.

This book sets out to tell another extraordinary story, one that's close to our hearts. Once again we turned to the photographer Bruna Rotunno, whose images magnificently capture the graceful beauty and allure of this legendary creature, as well as the time-honored rituals that have paid tribute to the Queen of the Andes since the days of the Incas.

Sergio and Pier Luigi Loro Piana

Edited by
Loro Piana Marketing Communication

Text by
Arianna Piazza

Graphic project and layout
Gritti Morlacchi & Schirmer, Milan

Editorial coordination
Eva Vanzella

Copy editor
Emanuela di Lallo

Translation
Anna Carruthers

Photography credits
© 2013 Bruna Rotunno

First published in Italy in 2013 by Skira Editore S.p.A.
Palazzo Casati Stampa
via Torino 61, 20123 Milan, Italy
www.skira.net

© 2013 Loro Piana S.p.A.
© 2013 Skira editore, Milan

Printed and bound in Italy.

ISBN: 978-88-572-1386-6

Distributed in USA, Canada, Central & South America by Rizzoli International
Publications, Inc., 300 Park Avenue South, New York, NY 10010, USA.
Distributed elsewhere in the world by Thames and Hudson Ltd., 181A High Holborn,
London WC1V 7QX, United Kingdom.

Contents

The Queen of the Andes

In the days of the Inca Empire, the Emperor ruled over men, forests and mountains, overlooked by the stern, watchful gaze of the Sun god, Inti and the goddess Pachamama, Mother Earth. Yet on the highest peaks, there lived a graceful, regal creature in possession of special powers, the stuff of legend, magic, and nature: the vicuña, Queen of the Andes. The vicuña is the smallest member of the alpaca, llama and guanaco family, around a meter tall at the shoulder and rarely weighing more than 50 kilograms. This shy, graceful camelid has inspired legends and stories, achieving mythical status since it could not be hunted and the sumptuous fiber obtained from its fleece was only available to the Emperor and his family.

In the days of the Incas there were millions of vicuñas grazing freely on the steep slopes of the Andes. They were thought to have magical powers granted by the gods: people believed they were reincarnations of the dead, capable of appeasing the god Inti to ensure warmth and fertility on earth. Legend had it that the vicuña originated from water, and would take refuge in water to escape from anyone wishing to tame it. Indeed vicuñas have always lived wild, dominating the bitterly cold Andean plateaus with natural grace. Their soft fleece affords extraordinary insulation, enabling the animals to survive the freezing nights and long winters. The legendary Queen of the Andes is known as "The Gold of the Puna" in Argentina, and indeed, here the vicuña's coat is lighter in color, with golden nuances. This is the result of a natural selection process, favoring the survival of the animals that blended in better with the cold, subtle colors of the land in northern Argentina.

In this area the species has proved particularly vulnerable to predators, with the most deadly, as often, being man. At the end of the fifteenth century there were more than one million vicuñas in South America; a century later the figure fell to just a few thousand, following the massacre carried out by Francisco Pizarro's Spanish *conquistadores*, eager to trade in the divine fiber made from its fleece. Since then, despite numerous conservation attempts implemented by various governments, starting with the laws passed by Simón Bolívar in 1825, poaching has continued at an alarming rate. In the 1960s the number of vicuñas fell to no more than five thousand, bringing the animal to the brink of extinction.

For this reason, in 1976 the Washington Convention (CITES) placed the vicuña on the list of protected species and, with the aim of discouraging poaching, completely banned any trading in its precious fiber. After the first reserves were set up and repopulation programs got under way, in 1987 the Peruvian government obtained authorization from CITES to start reintroducing small quantities of fiber onto the market, collected exclusively by shearing live animals. To ensure the success of the protection program throughout the country, the government recruited the local communities: by entrusting the care of the animals to local people in exchange for use of the fiber, the conservation program offered a valid and profitable alternative to illegal poaching. The Peruvian government also needed reputable, trusted partners to work with. After the first unsuccessful competition in 1992, in 1994 the International Vicuña Consortium, managed and promoted by Loro Piana, was awarded the exclusive rights to deal with vicuña fiber, while the Andean villagers were given permission to hold the animals in usufruct, in exchange for protecting them from poachers. Since then, with the support of responsible business partners such as Loro Piana, the conservation programs introduced by the Peruvian government and other South American countries, including Argentina, have effectively saved this proud, wild species, one that continues to represent an extraordinary celebration of freedom and nature.

The inhabitants of the mountain plateaus still believe in the magical properties of the vicuña:
legend has it that the animal is capable of transforming its precious fleece into gold.

With its long neck, pointed ears,
and big, deep eyes
set in a small and delicate head,
the vicuña is the undisputed Queen of the Andes.

The vicuña feeds on the scarce vegetation that manages to survive in the harsh conditions of the mountain plateaus and steppe.

From birth, after an eleven-month gestation period, baby vicuñas are ready to face the Puna.
The offspring stay with their mother for about a year and then form small flocks that roam wild across vast swathes of land.

The physical characteristics of the vicuña vary according to the climate.
The animals in Argentina are larger because they have more food and, above all, more water.

The vicuñas in Argentina have a delicate, light colored coat, the result of a natural selection process.
The ivory shades afford a better defence against predators, enabling the animals to blend into the cold hues of the Puna landscape.

According to ruling tradition,
the Andes people must always respect Pachamama,
Mother Earth, and the vicuña.
Transgressors are punished by the curse
of the shaking mountains and bad harvests until they learn
to respect animals and nature.

Ever on the lookout for signals in its surroundings and a fast mover,
the vicuña lives to about the age of 12.
A year after birth the young animals separate into flocks of males and females that live close by but apart.

In Peru, the Hanan Wanka native people
believe that their ancestors come from Ñahuinpuquio,
the lake on the mountain plateau where the vicuñas rise from the water.
The implacable Coquena,
the legendary guardian of the plateaus and the snowfields,
protects the vicuñas by guiding them to new pastureland…

The vicuñas live in flocks at altitudes that range from 3,800 to 4,800 meters in Peru, Bolivia, Argentina, Chile, and Colombia.
In spite of the lack of oxygen, they are fast movers.
The physical characteristics of the animal, and its blood, rich in sugars and red blood cells which absorb
and store oxygen, make it the undisputed sovereign of these peaks.

Following pages
A flock of vicuñas in the Dr. Franco Loro Piana Reserve. Each animal requires at least a hectare of land to survive.

THE PEOPLE OF THE PERUVIAN ANDES

The first organized cultures in the area now known as Peru date back to long before the arrival of the Incas. The Chimú, Chancay, Wari, and Nazca peoples all inhabited Peru's varied lands, leaving behind extraordinary structures, sophisticated crafted artifacts, refined sculptures and mysterious lost cities. The Incas were undoubtedly the most famous and successful empire of South America, dominating an extraordinary but often treacherous landscape in the fifteenth century with their wide roads, efficient administration and ingenious people. Their sovereign was a descendant of the Sun god, who perspired droplets of gold on the earth. His Moon queen wept tears of silver over the Empire – a land rich in natural resources, but difficult to inhabit with its harsh climate, blustering winds and scarce oxygen at high altitudes.

Despite the absence of writing – with all forms of information being communicated orally – the widespread road system which linked the mountains to the coast, and the country's legal organization and solid central government guaranteed a lengthy period of unity in an area strongly characterized by diverse regional identities. With the arrival of Francisco Pizarro's Spanish invaders, however, most of the native population was wiped out by epidemics and the ruthless regime of slavery that was imposed. Today Peru has a fairly heterogeneous population of different ethnic groups and cultures, a legacy of its past. The Catholicism introduced by the *conquistadores* spread throughout the country, but never completely replaced the ancient religions connected to the pagan gods of the earth and the sky. The Mother Earth figure of Pachamama often overlapped and merged into that of the Virgin Mary, while above all among the *campesinos*, legends as old as the hills continued to hold sway. The inhabitants of the rural mountainous areas used traditional farming techniques, growing potatoes and maize and rearing llamas, alpacas, sheep, and goats. Villagers were usually related on various levels and brought up the new generations by handing down the old traditional values.

In Peru the *campesinos* have the honor of tending to the animal that symbolizes the Andes, and that even appears on the nation's coat of arms: the vicuña. In its efforts to save this precious camelid from extinction the government also sought the help of local people, who are entrusted with the task of ensuring the animals' survival. In exchange the *campesino* communities are granted the right to the income generated by selling the fleeces. The shearing is strictly controlled and carried out using the ancient methods of the Incas, with the commitment to safeguard the animals and protect them from poaching. Loro Piana has been involved in this preservation program for the last thirty years, committed to respecting the Andean people and their love for their own land and history, revived in the ancient shearing ritual, and guaranteeing that the animals can live wild: a success story that embodies the social and cultural resurgence of an entire community.

Peru is strongly tied to its traditions, which are preserved and cherished
by its native people, who make up nearly half the population.

The *campesino*s: wide, brightly-colored skirts, hats
pushed down over weather-beaten faces,
wrapped up in cloaks to protect them against a sudden cold snap
or to carry children and supplies on their shoulders.

Due to the extreme climate conditions, few people live on the mountain plateaus.
Only the descendants of the Incas venture into this impervious land.

About half of the full-blooded natives are *campesinos*
living in rural areas where they farm and raise livestock.

The bright colors of the traditional garments
break up the neutral palette of the mountain landscape.
The art of weaving is a precious,
ancient local heritage.

The inhabitants of the Andes live at one with nature, guided by an abiding respect for the earth and the sky.

Religious traditions coexist in a curious mix
of the sacred and profane.
Ancestral beliefs merge with Catholicism
and are shrouded in the mystery of legends.

The Andean natives speak *Quechua*, the ancient official language of the Incas,
which boasts a surprising number of dialects.

Men, women and children prepare to celebrate the *chaccu* ritual with songs and dances, and the *pagapu*,
the ancient ceremony devoted to the Mother Earth Pachamama and the Andean gods who protect their animals.

The *chaccu* is just one of Peru's many folk celebrations connected to the history and legends of these mountains.
The traditional costumes take the Andean people back to the days in which the Apus gods,
the spirits of the peaks, stood watch over animals and the natural world.

PERUVIAN LANDSCAPES:
THE DR. FRANCO LORO PIANA RESERVE

Since the first exploration of Machu Picchu in 1911 historians, archaeologists and scientists have been trying to reconstruct traces of the extraordinary civilizations that inhabited one of South America's most fascinating countries. The third largest nation in Latin America, Peru boasts an incomparable variety of landscapes. Its sandy, desert coastline and lush Amazonian jungle are divided by the spectacular wilderness of the Andes, the country's majestic, imposing backbone that rises up to challenge the sky. The mountain range runs from north to south, reaching impressive heights. At 6,768 meters, Huascarán is the highest peak in the earth's tropical regions. At these altitudes, the lunar-like landscape is icy and silent, swathed in an extreme, rarefied atmosphere. Between 3,000 and 4,000 meters the land is farmed, and it is here that most of the natives live – in villages where time appears to have stood still. Centuries of history come alive here, in the intense, proud faces of the descendants of Peru's ancient peoples.

A plane trip over this area reveals one of the most incredible sights that this land has to offer: an expanse of 500 square kilometers marked by lines carved into the earth to form enormous animal shapes. These are the famed Nazca lines: monkeys, lizards, spiders, and other animals up to 300 meters long, which can only be seen from the air. The mystery of their meaning and how they were created has been puzzling scientists for more than a century, with most theories merely opening up further layers of mystery.

The animal species that live in these lands possess special characteristics to help them survive the extremely harsh climate. Vicuña, llama, alpaca, guanaco, and condor all live wild in the Pampa Galeras reserve between Nazca and Cuzco, set up by the Peruvian government to protect the sacred animal of the Andes from extinction. Established in 1967, the reserve occupies a total of 6,500 hectares, where the vicuñas can live in their natural habitat, strictly monitored. This park has become the national symbol of the fight to preserve this extraordinary animal.

Loro Piana, which has long been working with the Peruvian government to combat the indiscriminate poaching of the Queen of the Andes, re-affirmed its commitment by purchasing more than 2,000 hectares of land in the areas of Ñahuinpuquio and Yanaranra, 80 kilometers from the Pampa Galeras National Reserve. This plot is part of a private natural reserve named after Franco Loro Piana, the father of Sergio and Pier Luigi, the company's current CEOs. Here, in conjunction with the local communities, an effective system for safeguarding and monitoring the animals has been introduced. The program has aided the reproduction of the species, with the result that the number of vicuñas originally registered in the reserve has doubled in little more than five years.

Heading south, the mountains plunge steeply for thousands of meters, creating terrifying canyons that penetrate deep into the heart of a land dominated by snowy peaks. Peru's breathtaking landscapes go from summits whipped by biting winds – where conditions range from blistering sun to freezing winters, and even just breathing is difficult – to lush forests of impenetrable vegetation, and dry, rocky deserts: a country undisputedly dominated by the natural elements.

The sign marks the entrance to the Dr. Franco Loro Piana Reserve:
more than 2,000 hectares of land in the areas of Ñahuinpuquio and Yanaranra,
80 kilometers from Pampa Galeras.

Vicuñas running free among the rocks in the Dr. Franco Loro Piana Reserve.

With the support of Loro Piana, the Peruvian government and local communities have committed to safeguarding the vicuña, whose population in Peru now stands at over 180,000.

In this land nature can be merciless and water is very often in short supply.
Here in the reserve, water is a resource of inestimable value that guarantees the health and survival of the vicuñas and other species.

In Yanaranra Loro Piana has created areas for observing, studying, and safeguarding the vicuña.

A park ranger observes and monitors the area at dawn.

A lone vicuña dominates the rocks
in the area that Loro Piana gifted to the Queen of the Andes
in order to preserve its wild beauty.

On the windswept steppe there is no shelter from the blinding sun.

Typical of the arid steppe, the vegetation of the Puna grassland is sparse and low-growing.
There are many species of cacti here capable of withstanding the extreme range of temperatures and the harsh climate of the Andes.

THE CHACCU

The graceful symbol of a life lived free in the wilds, the vicuña enjoyed special protection among the ancient peoples of the Andes. Vicuñas were safeguarded by laws that prevented them from being hunted or cruelly sheared. Indeed for the Incas the process of gathering the fiber was a genuine collective ritual. Known as *chaccu* or *chakku*, it involved entire communities and was carried out before the Emperor in person. It only took place once every four years to enable the animals to grow enough fleece to shear and make sure they were protected from the harsh climate of the Puna.

The *chaccu* followed a precise ritual: a throng of 20 or 30 thousand men would drive the huge flocks of vicuñas along the steep slopes towards the shearing enclosure, waving colored ropes in the air, shouting and clapping their hands. In the baking sun at the end of the Andean summer, hundreds of vicuñas would gallop wildly across the dry, treeless lands, raising huge clouds of dust. When they made their appearance, entire villages would celebrate the delicate shearing process with dances, songs and merrymaking. After being sheared, the animals were immediately freed once again.

This method for obtaining the fiber of the gods was abandoned with the arrival of Francisco Pizarro's *conquistadores*: in order to get their hands on the silk of the New World quickly and in great quantities, the invaders embarked on a veritable massacre of the vicuña. Indiscriminate poaching, also carried out by criminal organizations active in contraband, continued up to the 1990s, in spite of the numerous measures implemented by South American governments and the creation of the first protected natural reserves.

Thanks to its work with the local communities and reputable international partners such as Loro Piana, the Peruvian government succeeded in saving the species from extinction, and in doing so, preserved the accompanying traditions and rituals. In 1994 Loro Piana was granted the right to reintroduce the vicuña fiber onto the market, and since then the company has continued to promote it and educate the markets on the use of fiber obtained only from cruelty-free, controlled shearing – a condition that adds further value to this intrinsically precious fiber. Fourteen years later, in 2008, this ongoing commitment came to fruition with the creation of the Dr. Franco Loro Piana Reserve, where in the same year, Loro Piana had the honor of organizing its very first *chaccu*. This ancestral ritual embodies the rich identity and heritage of the local people. Loro Piana, the Peruvian government and the *campesino* communities have been working together for around thirty years now, with a shared commitment to protect and develop this time-honored heritage and tradition, preserving a living legend. The program for controlling and ensuring responsible trading of this raw material is about more than just restoring the life cycle and population of the species: it means saving a tradition, a legendary practice that unites whole villages in a genuine celebration of the gifts of nature.

Preparing for the *chaccu* takes several days:
the vicuñas' territory is observed,
and prayers are made to the gods of the mountains.
Colored ribbons and nets mark the route that will take
the Queen of the Andes to her encounter with man.

A group of *campesinos* arrive at the Dr. Franco Loro Piana Reserve,
where the ancient ritual of the *chaccu*, with its songs and dances, will be performed.

The women prepare for the *chaccu* ritual,
donning the colorful traditional dress of the Ayacucho region.

The *chaccu* is a day of celebration, steeped in legends and tradition,
where dances and songs revive ancient rituals
to honor this precious ancestral legacy.
Music from the harps echoes throughout the mountains.

Previous pages
The ceremony: decked in condor feathers, the Machocc wears wooden shoes for the ritual dance,
while Huaylia girls wave sticks decorated with geometric patterns before taking part in the *chaccu*.

Tijera dancers celebrate Mother Earth Pachamama. In Andean mythology they represent the clash between the native religion and Catholicism brought by the Spanish invaders.

Everyone gets involved in preparations for the ceremony. A rope more than 2,000 meters long is laid out and the *bandoleras* are tied to it to mark the route the vicuñas will take to the shearing enclosure.

The *bandoleras*, strips of colored cloth, prevent the vicuñas from changing direction and guide them towards the shearing area. Music and songs accompany the ritual.

Previous pages
The vicuñas begin their descent from the mountain tops, guided by a human chain along the route.

Quick and agile, the Queens of the Andes leap between rocks and steppe, heading for the corridor that leads to the pens.

The vicuñas are about to reach their destination.

Men, women and children wave the *bandoleras* and accompany the vicuñas along the colorful cordons,
in a festive atmosphere that celebrates nature.

The *chaccu* is almost over.
The vicuñas are corraled into the enclosure, where they are treated
with the utmost care. Just a few more minutes
and the Andes will have their queens back.

Once the vicuñas have been rounded up, *campesinos* immediately free the younger ones and those not yet ready to be sheared. Those deemed suitable are gently made to lie on a mat and sheared as quickly as possible and then let free to roam again.

Pier Luigi Loro Piana holding the first fleece
sheared during the *chaccu* held in 2008 on the Dr. Franco Loro Piana Reserve.

The unique softness of the fiber can be felt immediately.
The vicuñas are free to roam again,
leaving man with their rare and precious gift.

The Fiber of the Gods

Among the ancient peoples of Peru, society was strictly regulated by a set of conventions and practices connected to the individual's *status*. Fabrics, garments and ornaments were all part of this complex hierarchy. The fiber, colors, patterns, and even the cut of garments differed for soldiers, the aristocracy, the clergy or the Emperor. The most precious fabrics were created by young girls dear to Inti, the Sun god, in the Akllawasi, a place of meditation and study set aside exclusively for them. These chosen few were the only people authorized to touch and work with the world's rarest, finest fiber, reserved solely for the Emperor's personal use: that of the legendary vicuña. The fabrics made from the fiber of the Queen of the Andes were woven using manual techniques of astounding excellence, comparable to the precision of a mechanical loom.

The vicuña possesses the finest fiber that can legally be harvested from an adult animal: an average of only 12–13 micron in diameter. This impalpable raw material is the result of the species' natural process of adaptation to the harsh conditions in the Andes. To survive the freezing winters and scorching summers, this tenacious camelid has developed an underfleece, in a characteristic golden color, that is made up of ultrafine, short and extremely dense fibers, with extraordinary thermoregulating properties. The outer coat instead presents long, strong hairs that protect the animals from the elements. This legendary fleece shines in the blistering sun of the high peaks in a range of warm, intense shades: *vermejo, aleonado, ladrillo,* and *rosaseca* – namely golden chestnut to bright fawn. In Argentina, where the climate is even more extreme, the fiber is exceptionally fine and lighter in color, almost white, blending into the glacial hues of the Puna.

Gathering and processing this extremely rare, exclusive fiber is a time-consuming process that respects tradition. The animals are only sheared once every two years, with an adult producing around 250 grams of hair; after being dehaired (the process to remove the coarser guard hairs) this amounts to just 120–150 grams. The result is a unique fabric: supremely light, incomparably soft and magnificently warm. The devastating poaching of the vicuña to get hold of this treasure risked driving the species to extinction and occasioning the loss of centuries of tradition. As a result, in the 1970s trading in the fiber was banned. Loro Piana has appreciated this ultrafine fleece since the 1950s, prior to the vicuña becoming a protected species. In line with the firm's ongoing research into raw materials of authentic quality, it never lost the hope in one day being able to deal with this legendary fiber.

Today Loro Piana is the number one manufacturer of this supreme material that is spun, woven, and crafted entirely in Italy. The company's commitment to excellence has granted it the privilege of working with the fiber of the gods, contributing to preserving the species, and discouraging all forms of poaching and contraband. Each garment in vicuña must be legally certified and accompanied with documentation that proves it comes from animals sheared live, in a completely traceable process. The Queen of the Andes continues to dress the world: as in the ancient Inca legends, nature yields unique and precious gifts to those who respect her.

The shearing and selection process still take place in the traditional manner,
entrusted to the experience and skill of the local population, in respect of a unique, highly prized material.

The dehairing, namely the removal of the coarse guard hairs, is done by hand.
It takes a week of work to dehair one kilogram of fiber, the equivalent to the fleece of four animals.

The privilege of divine sovereigns,
the legendary golden fleece is handled by experienced natives
who are the guardians of the vicuñas' gift.

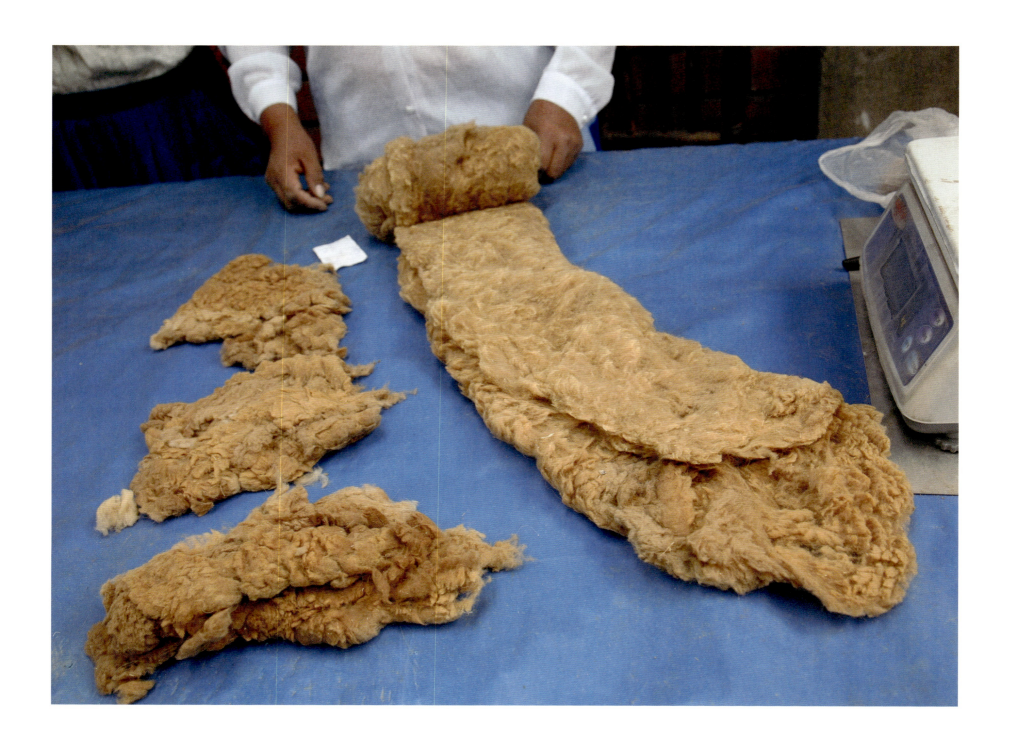

Each animal is sheared once every two years;
an adult produces around 250 grams of the precious fiber.

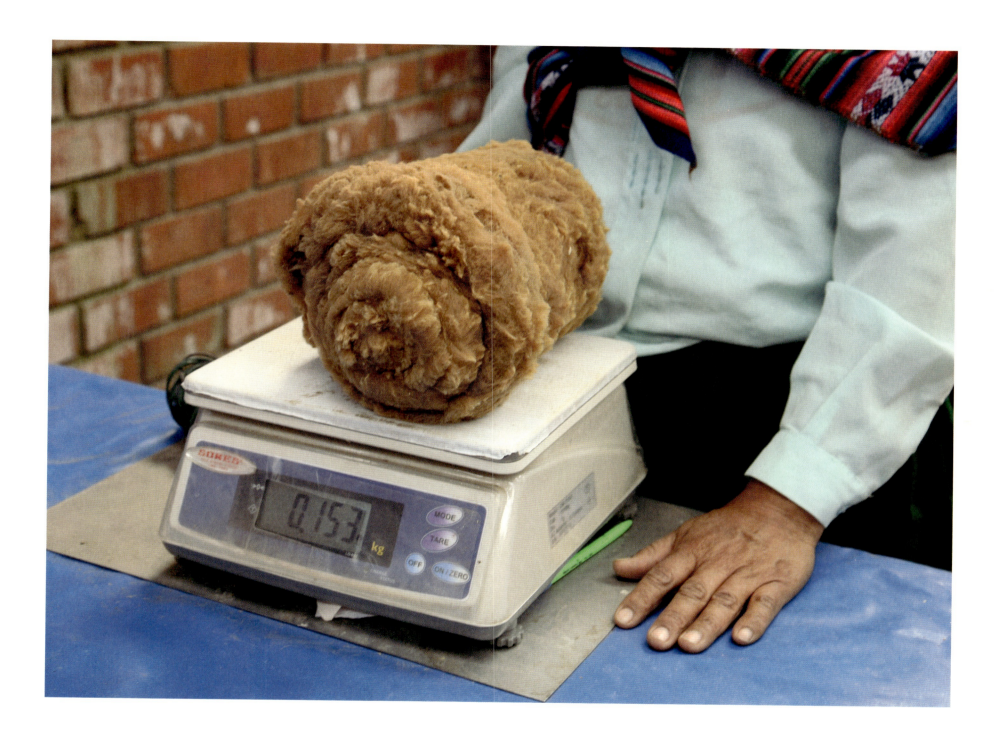

After the dehairing process, when the coarse guard hairs are separated from the finer, more valuable underfleece, the yield from each animal goes down to just 120–150 grams of light, soft, and durable fiber.

The coat of the vicuña is made up of coarser outer hairs and the light, extremely warm underfleece.

In Argentina's icy uplands the vicuña develops a warm and very fine underfleece
to withstand a harsh climate where temperatures can drop to minus 20 or 30 °C.

Against the glacial landscapes of Laguna Blanca,
the light colored coat of the Argentine vicuña blends in with the silvery nuances of the rocks and water.

Man's commitment to safeguarding the vicuña
has saved a natural heritage of inestimable value:
the prized fiber of its fleece
and its life running free in the wilderness.

THE LANDSCAPES OF ARGENTINA

In the Andes, the Puna grasslands extend southwards from Peru to Bolivia, Chile, and the north-western provinces of Argentina. The Puna region of Argentina lies in the province of Catamarca, between the department of Antofagasta de la Sierra and that of Belén. Little-known to tourists, these lands reveal breathtaking natural panoramas, ancient archaeological sites, and remote cities where folk traditions live on and time seems suspended. The landscape is arid and immobile, there is very little rain, and the difference between day- and night-time temperatures is extreme. In winter they can fall to minus 20 or 30 °C. Upon leaving the city of San Fernando del Valle de Catamarca, with its magnificent colonial architecture, and heading towards Antofagasta de la Sierra, the extremely harsh climate of the Puna begins to make itself felt. The vast, empty silences of this landscape are the realm of red and gray foxes, Andean wild cats, llamas, guanacos, and vicuñas.

As in Peru, the history of the legendary vicuña is associated with poaching on a devastating scale, which often goes unchecked due to the difficulty of policing such a vast, largely unpopulated area. Consequently, the animal has been at the risk of extinction. To protect the species, in 1979 the Laguna Blanca Biosphere Reserve was created, which in 1982 became part of UNESCO's "Man and Biosphere" project (MAB). Due to the rules set down by CITES, vicuñas now live wild, but protected, in an area of 770,000 hectares at an altitude that ranges from 3,200 to 5,500 meters above sea level, in the areas of Antofagasta de la Sierra and Belén.

In Argentina there are fewer vicuñas than in Peru, and unlike in Peru, they are not the property of the government or the local communities; they are simply viewed as part of the fauna present in the area. However, the government is committed to protecting and safeguarding the species, and monitoring the shearing process, which must take place on live animals and using cruelty-free methods. The huge size of the area means that private commitment is important. Operating in organized structures, the companies involved monitor and count the animals, and have the permission of the government of the Catamarca province to shear the vicuñas that settle in the areas they are responsible for.

On the wave of its experience in Peru, Loro Piana recently began to operate in Argentina, purchasing a majority share in a structure situated in the department of Belén, with rights to an area of around 85,000 hectares on the edge of the Laguna Blanca Reserve. Loro Piana is now using its experience in the protection of the species in this new area, taking a responsible, long-term view of the future of these lands and their resources, and with the guarantee of trading in a fiber obtained only in the total respect of life and nature.

The shearing is carried out with a view to ensuring a sustainable supply of this rare, highly prized excellence. Those responsible for the shearing keep the largest amount of the resulting fiber, while the remaining part goes to the government of the Catamarca province, which distributes it among local artisans. The latter spin, weave and work the vicuña fiber, keeping the traditions alive and producing the legendary local ponchos, which even have their own festival (Fiesta Nacional del Poncho), held for more than 400 years in the very province of Catamarca. Vicuña ponchos, worn by the *caudillos* and important people who have shaped the history of the country, have become a symbol of wealth and prestige. In this part of the world vicuña is a gift of nature connected to history and traditions, and to those who honor the bounty of the earth and the skies.

Dazzling, cold colors, and vast, uninhabited swathes of land. In the background, the Cerros de Curuto mountains as seen from the Pasto Ventura plain. The snowy peaks alternate with sandy dunes in unreal hues.

The dizzying canyon of Barranca Larga makes way for the tiny, precious lakes of Aguada de Randolfo,
in the Belén department.

Thanks to the work of Loro Piana, on the estate between El Peñón and Pasto Ventura
there are now over 4,500 vicuñas registered, out of a total of nearly 40,000 head in all of Argentina.
The vicuña's light colored coat and incredibly soft fiber developed as a response to this harsh, icy land.